IN A PICKLE

AND OTHER FUNNY IDIOMS

BY MARVIN TERBAN

ILLUSTRATED BY GIULIO MAESTRO

CLARION BOOKS
NEW YORK

To my wife Karen,
who has gotten me out
of many a pickle

Clarion Books
a Houghton Mifflin Company imprint
215 Park Avenue South, New York, NY 10003
Text copyright © 1983 by Marvin Terban
Illustrations copyright © 1983 by Giulio Maestro
Printed in the USA

Library of Congress Cataloging in Publication Data
Terban, Marvin.
In a pickle, and other funny idioms.
Summary: Thirty common English phrases, such as
"a chip off the old block" and "don't cry over spilled milk"
are illustrated and explained.
1. English language—Terms and phrases—Juvenile
literature.   [1. English language—Terms and phrases]
I. Maestro, Giulio, ill.   II. Title.
PE1689.T44 1983 428.1   82-9585
ISBN 0-89919-153-3

Paperback ISBN 0-89919-164-9
EB 20 19 18 17

Idioms

Idioms are groups of words that really don't mean what they say. What they actually say can sometimes seem silly, as the pictures in this book show.

Idioms are confusing because each one has a special meaning. If you don't know the special meaning, you won't understand what someone is saying.

This book tells you the real and special meanings of thirty popular idioms. Not all word experts agree on where certain idioms come from or even on exactly what some of them mean. But here are the explanations most people know and accept.

If you want to find out about other idioms you have heard or read, the books listed on the last page may help you.

Now she is really in a pickle!

IDIOM

In a pickle

MEANING

In trouble. In an unpleasant situation.

Years ago, people didn't have refrigerators to help keep vegetables and meat from spoiling. They sometimes put them in a large barrel filled with vinegar or brine. This was called "pickling." Imagine someone sitting on the lid of a pickle barrel. Ooops! He falls in. Now he's in big trouble.

Whenever he performs, he gets butterflies in the stomach!

IDIOM

Butterflies in the stomach

MEANING

A weird feeling caused by fear or nervousness

A big spelling test is about to start. Or you're stepping up to bat. Or it's your turn to go on stage to sing.

You're tense. You're scared. You feel a fluttery sensation in your stomach. Are butterflies in there? Of course not! Your nervousness just makes it feel as if a million wings were flapping inside of you.

She certainly opened a can
of worms this time!

IDIOM

Open a can of worms

MEANING

Start a lot of trouble
that will be hard to stop

If you actually opened a can of worms, all the worms would get out and you wouldn't be able to get them back in. They would be squirming all over, and some people would be running and squealing. You certainly would have started a lot of trouble, wouldn't you?

Today, people use this expression to mean causing trouble that is difficult to handle.

"Every time you go to a garage sale, you come home with another white elephant!"

IDIOM

White elephant

MEANING

A totally useless possession
that you'd like to get rid of

A long time ago in Siam (now Thailand), a white elephant was a sacred animal.

When the King of Siam was angry at someone, he gave him a white elephant as a "present." The white elephant could never be made to work. It would live only in pampered luxury. Its new owner would probably run out of money caring for it. Some present!

Today at a flea market or school fair, you might see people selling "white elephants." Don't look for any light-colored pachyderms. White elephants are just some junk that people don't want anymore and would like to sell to you.

"Swim away! Don't bury
your head in the sand!"

IDIOM

Bury your head in the sand

MEANING

Pretend that danger doesn't exist
when it really does

For a long time people had the mistaken idea that the world's biggest bird, the ostrich, buried its head in the sand to hide from danger. People believed the ostrich thought that if it couldn't see its enemy, the enemy couldn't see it.

The ostrich is really an excellent fighter. If you got one angry, it would fight you with its beak and powerful feet.

If you see an ostrich with its head down, it's not hiding from its enemies. It's just looking for seeds or berries to eat.

"You shouldn't have counted your
chickens before they hatched!"

IDIOM

Don't count your chickens before
they hatch.

MEANING

Don't make plans based upon something
that hasn't happened yet.

Not all plans turn out the way we think they
will. For example, not all eggs hatch. If a
farmer counts five eggs in a nest, it doesn't
mean he's going to have five baby chicks. If
he advertises FIVE CHICKS FOR SALE, he may
be in for a disappointing surprise if only three
eggs hatch.

"There he goes again, putting the
cart before the horse!"

IDIOM

To put the cart before the horse

MEANING

To get the order of things backward

If you try to walk a tightrope before you've taken any tightrope walking lessons, or if you eat dessert first, then the main course, you've got things in reverse order. You're "putting the cart before the horse."

A farmer who actually put his horse behind the wagon instead of in front of it wouldn't get very far, would he?

"He's always putting his foot
in his mouth!"

IDIOM

To put your foot into your mouth

MEANING

To say something that you
shouldn't have said

If you don't watch where you're walking, you
could put your foot right into something dis-
agreeable. If you don't watch what you're
saying, you could say something that might
offend someone.

Naturally your foot wouldn't actually be inside your mouth when you were committing
this social blunder. But the idea is the same.
Your mouth is where the unpleasant words
came from, and because you weren't careful,
you "put your foot" right into it.

He keeps beating around
the bush!

IDIOM

To beat around the bush

MEANING

To avoid coming directly to the point

Suppose you are a hunter of small animals. One runs into the bushes. To get it out, you should beat on the bush with a stick. But you don't actually do that. You beat all around the bush but not right on it.

If you talk all around a subject without ever coming to the point, you're "beating around the bush."

Things just seem to go in one
ear and out the other!

IDIOM

In one ear and out the other

MEANING

Going through the mind
without leaving an impression

There's plenty inside a person's head. Nothing could really go "in one ear and out the other." But if someone isn't paying attention to what is being said, then words do seem to pass right through that person's head without being heard.

Being caught up a tree
is no fun!

IDIOM

Up a tree

MEANING

In difficulty. In trouble.

This phrase comes from raccoon hunting. Dogs would chase a raccoon and force it up a tree. Then it was helpless.

Have you ever felt trapped in an impossible situation? You just couldn't think how to get out of it. Then you know how it feels to be "up a tree."

"I said to keep your
shirt on!"

IDIOM

Keep your shirt on.

MEANING

Stay calm.

Years ago shirts used to shrink after they were washed and became tighter. If a man got into a fight, his tight shirt would make it difficult for him to move his arms freely. So men took their shirts off at the beginning of a fight, so they could throw some good punches.

Today, if somebody tells you to "keep your shirt on," he or she is saying, "Don't get angry. Stay calm."

"Her eyes are bigger than
her stomach!"

IDIOM

Your eyes are bigger than your stomach.

MEANING

You ask for a lot of food,
but then you can't eat it all.

In real life, of course, your stomach is much, much bigger than your eyes. But suppose you ask for all this food: two hot dogs, a slice of pizza, a glass of soda, a bag of popcorn, an ice-cream cone, and a large chocolate doughnut. It looks good. But you can't possibly finish all that because your stomach is full. You would realize what it means when someone says, "Your eyes are bigger than your stomach."

He got it straight from
the horse's mouth!

IDIOM

Straight from the horse's mouth

MEANING

Information gotten from the most reliable source

This is old horse slang. Suppose you want to buy a horse and you ask how old it is. How can you be sure the seller is telling the truth?

Easy. Just look into the horse's mouth. If you know a lot about horses, you can tell approximately how old a horse is by the size and shape of its teeth. And you could be sure of your information because you got it "straight from the horse's mouth."

"He's giving him the
cold shoulder!"

IDIOM

To give someone the cold shoulder

MEANING

To show someone he's not welcome.
To rebuff or reject him

In the time of knights in shining armor, a host would welcome a traveling knight with a large, hot meal.

But if a common traveler came knocking on the castle door, he was often given a cold shoulder of mutton (sheep). When the guest saw this cold piece of bony, leftover meat on his plate, he got the hint that his visit was un-welcome.

That was a close shave!

IDIOM

A close shave

MEANING

A narrow escape from danger

Look closely at the edge of a razor blade. Careful! It's sharp. People glide it over their faces and other parts of their bodies to get a smooth shave.

But one slip, and ouch! A painful cut.

There's just a tiny difference between a close shave and a nasty gash. So when there's just a narrow margin between safety and danger, and you escape, you've had a "close shave."

You should beware of
crocodile tears!

IDIOM

Crocodile tears

MEANING

Make believe sorrow

There is an old story about a crocodile that sobbed like a person in great trouble. Someone heard the phony moans and went to help the poor "man" in distress. *Gulp!* The crocodile ate him up.

Today we call any fake crying "crocodile tears."

"You really laid an egg
this time!"

IDIOM

To lay an egg

MEANING

To be a big failure

This is old sports slang. A zero up on the scoreboard was sometimes referred to as a "goose egg." So a ball team that hasn't scored a single point has laid an "egg" on the scoreboard.

Today this idiom often refers to performers in a show. When an actor or a singer does an act that flops, we say that he or she has "laid an egg."

She got up on the wrong
side of the bed!

IDIOM

To get up on the wrong side of the bed

MEANING

To be grumpy

The ancient Romans were very superstitious. They thought it was extremely unlucky to get out of bed on the left side. (The Latin word for *left* is *sinister,* which means "bad" or "evil.")

The right side of the bed was the safe, correct side. So if you absentmindedly got out on the left side, you would probably have a terribly unlucky day. That would certainly put you into a nasty mood, wouldn't it?

"Look out! He's flying
off the handle!"

IDIOM

To fly off the handle

MEANING

To explode into anger
and lose control

If you were building something and the head
of your hammer suddenly flew off its handle,
it could hurt somebody badly. If a person gets
furiously angry and dangerously out of control, we say he "flew off the handle."

"There she goes again,
putting on the dog!"

IDIOM

Putting on the dog

MEANING

Acting fancy. Putting on
a flashy display.

About a hundred years ago, Americans who
wanted to be accepted by the upper classes
copied a custom from rich Europeans. They
spent huge sums of money to buy fancy little
dogs to put on their laps, just for show.

Today if someone tries to act fancy, we say he
or she is "putting on the dog."

"Why you're just a chip off
the old block!"

IDIOM

A chip off the old block

MEANING

A child who looks or acts
like one of his or her parents

A woodcutter takes an axe and chops a piece of wood from a large block. The small chip looks very much like the big block. A child who looks very much like a parent is like that "chip off the old block." Same coloring. Same material.

You never know who has
a skeleton in the closet!

IDIOM

A skeleton in the closet

MEANING

A secret that could ruin
your reputation

There is an old story about someone who searched all over the world for a person with a perfect reputation. At last the searcher found a woman who seemed to have no worries and no secrets. But what did the searcher find hanging in her closet? A skeleton! Her fine reputation was ruined.

If you have a secret, no matter how small, that could spoil your good name, that's the "skeleton in your closet."

She threw the book at him!

IDIOM

To throw the book at someone

MEANING

To give someone the worst possible
punishment for the crime committed

Judges often have to look in law books to find
out what kinds of punishments they can give
for certain crimes.

If a judge imposes the maximum sentence on
someone convicted of a crime, we say that the
judge has "thrown the book" (meaning the
whole law book) at the guilty person.

He let the cat out
of the bag!

IDIOM

To let the cat out of the bag

MEANING

To reveal a secret, usually by accident

In old England, people at country fairs used to buy little pigs in bags. Sometimes a dishonest seller would stick a cat into the bag instead of a pig. When the buyer opened the bag and let the cat out, the secret was revealed.

Today we use this expression whenever someone tells a secret, usually without meaning to.

"It's no use crying
over spilled milk!"

IDIOM

Don't cry over spilled milk.

MEANING

It's useless to cry about
what can't be undone.

If you knock over a glass of milk, crying might make you feel better, but your tears won't get the milk back into the glass.

If something bad happens and there's no way to make it right again, tears are sometimes a comfort, but they aren't a solution to the problem.

He keeps getting into
everyone's hair!

IDIOM

To get into everyone's hair

MEANING

To keep bothering people

If something got into your hair—gum, sticky candy, paint, spaghetti sauce, glue—it would be hard to get out, and you certainly would be annoyed.

You can "get into someone's hair" when you keep bothering a person, even if he is bald!

She's always a wet blanket!

IDIOM

To be a wet blanket

MEANING

To be a spoilsport. To discourage
someone's plans.

A person can sometimes smother a small fire
by tossing a wet blanket over it.

Suppose you're excited about doing something that you think will be fun. But your
friend says it would be boring. Your friend is
being a "wet blanket" because he or she is
dampening your enthusiasm.

She took the words right
out of his mouth!

IDIOM

To take the words right out of someone's
mouth

MEANING

To say exactly what someone
was just going to say

Suppose you're thinking, It's a beautiful day,
and you're just going to say, It's a beautiful
day, but before you do, someone else says,
"It's a beautiful day." That person took the
words right out of your mouth.

He's simply sitting on
top of the world!

IDIOM

Sitting on top of the world

MEANING

Feeling extremely happy because of something you have accomplished

Suppose you've just climbed a high mountain and you're sitting at the top, looking down at the world below. Or you're an astronaut up in space watching the Earth float by.

You feel that you have done something wonderful! Marvelous! Terrific! You feel happier than you've ever felt before.

Whenever someone has that great feeling, we say, "He's sitting on top of the world!"

A Selection of Other Books About Idioms

Concise Dictionary of English Idioms by William Freeman, third edition revised and edited by Brian Phythian, The Writer, Inc., Boston, Mass., 1978.

Dictionary of American Idioms by Maxine Tull Boatner and John Edward Gates, Barron's Educational Series, Inc., Woodbury, N.Y., 1975.

Handbook of American Idioms and Idiomatic Usage by Harold C. Whitford and Robert J. Dixson, Regents Publishing Company, Inc., New York, 1973.

Handy Book of Commonly Used American Idioms by Solomon Wiener, Regents Publishing Company, Inc., New York, 1981.

Heavens to Betsy and Other Curious Sayings by Charles Earle Funk, Harper & Row, New York, 1955.

A Hog on Ice and Other Curious Expressions by Charles Earle Funk, Harper & Row, New York, 1948.